# How to survive
# RETIREMENT

Clive Whichelow & Mike Haskins

Illustrations by Kate Rochester

summersdale

HOW TO SURVIVE RETIREMENT

Summersdale Publishers Ltd
46 West Street
Chichester
West Sussex
PO19 1RP
UK

www.summersdale.com

Printed and bound in China

ISBN: 978-1-84953-138-2

Oct. 2013

To..... Dad

with love

From..... Clare + John

XXX

Other titles in this series:

*How to Survive Marriage*
*How to Survive Parenthood*
*How to Survive University*

# INTRODUCTION

Standing on the threshold of retirement, you may see it stretching before you in a vast featureless vista of nothingness or you might see it as a limitless wealth of new challenges, opportunities and quite a lot of nice cups of tea. However you look at it though, the secret to a happy retirement is not thinking of it as retirement at all — think of it as a new job!

Wanted: person aged 60-plus (now it's not often you see that in job descriptions is it, apart perhaps from those for high court judges?). Skills required – Time Management: being able to lie in bed till whatever time you fancy without feeling guilty; Business Awareness: not really giving a fig about the state of the nation; Professional Image: being able to stay in your dressing gown all day if you want to; Initiative: the ability to find ever more curious ways of occupying and entertaining yourself. Pay: negotiable.

Not bad, is it? And you can't be made redundant. Play your cards right and you could spin this out for decades.

# THE GOOD NEWS

From now on it's tea break time all day!

You are now free to confess you didn't
have a clue what you were doing at work
for the past 40 years

At last, you're your own boss!

# NEW FRIENDS YOU SHOULD TRY TO MAKE

The owners of your local cafes — they'll need to understand when you spin one cuppa out all afternoon

Your long-lost relatives who will find you now suddenly have time to stay 'for a few days or so' in their lovely rural or seaside retreats

A good new financial adviser to help sort out the pittance of a pension you got stuck with thanks to your previous financial adviser

The complaints officer at the local council – once you start looking, there will be so many things you will find to report

# TYPES OF RETIREE YOU COULD BE

Perky, all-action windsurfing, golf-playing, globetrotting gadabout who puts youngsters to shame

Thin-lipped, beige-wearing old crone who sees retirement as an excuse to take up moaning as a full-time job

The grey-haired supermarket trolley stacker who has discovered since retirement that they have to have a job — ANY sort of job!

# FIRST DAY DISASTERS TO AVOID

Forgetting to deactivate your early-morning alarm

Putting all the money you got from the equity release on your home on a horse running in the 3.30

Being over-friendly with the postman, window cleaner, telesales caller, etc. in your desperation to find someone to talk to

# GOOD AND BAD
# ROLE MODELS

| Good | Bad |
|---|---|
| People who enjoy cruising the world | People who are arrested for cruising up and down the high street |
| People who constantly do a lot of volunteer work | People who constantly need to be restrained by volunteers |
| People who devote their time to charity | People who devote their time to seeing what benefits they can claim |
| People who become pillars of their community | People who become pillocks of their community |

# SELF-HELP BOOKS YOU MIGHT WANT TO READ

*The Beginners' Guide to Living on One-Tenth of your Previous Income*

*Teach Yourself Pole Dancing for the Over Sixties*

*Think Yourself Rich*

*How to Whinge at Friends and*
*Influence People*

# FANTASIES YOU MAY START HAVING

The prime minister phones you up to beg you to come back to work, because without your input the economy is collapsing

Retirement is a sign from above that you are destined for better things

When you left work they needed three
people to replace you

# DOS AND DON'TS

Do attempt to keep in touch with the modern world

Don't wear a mobile phone attachment on your ear all the time — everyone will assume it's a hearing aid

Do try some exciting new experiences

Don't start going to the shops dressed in
rubber bondage wear

Do keep an active interest in what's going on in your neighbourhood

Don't get caught setting up surveillance equipment pointing at your neighbour's bathroom window

# BASIC LESSONS TO REMEMBER

Retirement doesn't have to be all golf, gardening and grandchildren — it could be fun, frolics and fabness too!

It's not the end of your working life, it's the start of your non-working life — enjoy!

When people want a famous pop musician to retire, they present them with a lifetime achievement award – look on your retirement as your lifetime achievement award!

You've done your bit for society, now it's someone else's turn

The more you keep yourself fit and healthy, the more you will get your money's-worth from your retirement

# EMBRACE RETIREMENT WITH A DOSE OF IRONY

Present your bus pass when boarding any form of transport from the miniature railway in the park to the space shuttle

Set the alarm clock for 11.00 a.m.

Get ready for work, go to your old workplace and feel the joy of being able to walk straight past it

When people phone you at home tell them
their calls may be recorded for training
and security purposes

Draw up an annual leave slip for yourself
with leave granted on every day of
the year

# READY RESPONSES FOR THINGS OTHERS WILL SAY TO YOU

'I bet you get a bit stuck for things to do during the day.'

'No, I don't want to paint your house for you.'

'Are you really sixty-five?'

'No, I'm twenty-seven but I just couldn't be bothered to work any longer.'

'What do you do with yourself all day?'
'Mainly, I answer stupid questions. Next!'

'So what's it like being able to sit with
your feet up doing nothing all day?'
'You tell me. You're the one who still goes
to work.'

# CHANGES THAT WILL OCCUR IN YOUR APPEARANCE

Men no longer need to worry about wearing the 'uniform' required at work, and instead don the official retiree's uniform of beige jacket and flat cap

Women no longer need to compete with their work colleagues and opt instead for the 'comfy look'

Slippers will become the most well-worn items of footwear in your wardrobe

# REALISTIC AND UNREALISTIC GOALS IN YOUR NEW LIFE

Realistic: Seeing a bit more of the world

Unrealistic: Living on a yacht in Monte Carlo surrounded by models and movie stars

Realistic: Developing a reputation as a source of wisdom and guidance

Unrealistic: Receiving regular calls for advice from the President of the USA, the Pope and the Dalai Lama

Realistic: Enjoying a full and
active retirement

Unrealistic: Still going for your daily
paragliding session on your
100th birthday

# SCIENCE AND NON-SCIENCE

By 2040 the number of people aged 65-plus will increase by 50 per cent — that's going to be one hell of a queue at the post office

Older people are more sensitive to the effects of alcohol — just as well when a couple of drinks costs half a week's pension

Although you may have heard of a pensions time-bomb, this does not mean that an explosive reaction will occur as soon as you cash your pension

In 20 years' time baby boomers (yes, that's us!) will have 90 per cent of the nation's disposable income — why do we have to wait 20 years?

Mammals from mice to elephants all live for about 800 million heartbeats — so don't exert yourself in later life in case you only have a couple of dozen left

# REALITY CHECK

Some of your friends may still be working, so don't rub it in about the tough day you've had visiting the National Trust tearooms

You may have a tad less cash than when you were working, so go easy on the luxury cruises

Everyone will now know how old you are, so put the baseball cap and skateboard away, you're fooling no one

Work expands to fill the time available, so trimming your toenails may now become an all-day job

You won't get rich watching daytime TV no matter how much you think it teaches you about the antiques and property markets

# ADVICE YOU WILL GET FROM OTHERS (AND CAN SAFELY IGNORE)

'Now you've finished work, why not do some voluntary work?'

'You should write your life story!'

'Take up golf; that'll be nice and relaxing'

# TRICKS TO MAKE OTHERS THINK YOU KNOW WHAT YOU ARE DOING

Offer counselling for newly-retired people

Always consult your diary when making arrangements (even if all the pages are blank)

Go out and do things you genuinely enjoy
doing each day

Tell people you're always far too busy to
see anything on daytime TV

Comment on the ups and downs of the stock market even if your life savings are stashed under the mattress

# MOMENTS YOU MAY HAVE TO CONTROL YOUR TEMPER

When bus drivers ask to see your pass
without even considering you might be
too young to have one

When your old office syndicate wins the
top prize on the lottery the week after
you leave

When you look at your pension statement

# ARGUMENTS YOU MAY FIND YOURSELF FALLING INTO

'You work to live not live to work!'

'Whoever set the amount for the pension never tried to live on it!'

'If people today had to do the amount of work I had to get through, they wouldn't know what had hit them!'

'I never thought I'd say it, but the teenagers are right — there isn't anything to do round here!'

# WHAT TO DO IF IT ALL GETS TOO MUCH

Retire to bed (preferably with someone else of a retiring nature)

Pretend all the things you have to do during the day are part of a job you've been given

Set up a holiday firm offering breaks to retirees fed up with retirement in the form of a couple of weeks a year back at work (for which they have to pay!)

Drive out in the rush hour and remind yourself that you used to endure this twice a day

Meet up with all your old workmates and listen to them grumbling about their jobs for half an hour

# TRY NOT TO THINK ABOUT THE MONEY YOU DIDN'T PUT AWAY

On an average wage, over your working life you should have earned over £1m. So where's it all gone?

You could have saved it all for your retirement and then squandered the lot on a gold-plated, diamond-encrusted stairlift

You could have bought five Rolls Royces — but as you'd have had no money for a house you would probably be living in one of them

You could have bought a little pub
especially for retirees called
The Pipe & Slippers

But just think, if you were a footballer
the money would only have lasted you a
couple of weeks

# THINGS YOU'LL FIND
# YOUSELF WORRYING ABOUT

| UNIMPORTANT | IMPORTANT |
|---|---|
| The fact that you don't have anything very pressing to do | That you haven't actually got out of bed for three days |
| Whether your other half will be able to put up with you all day | Whether your other half has gone back to work to escape you |
| Whether your old workplace is coping without you | That your old work colleagues haven't even noticed you've gone yet |
| Whether you manage to catch *Countdown* every afternoon | Whether you get out of bed in time to catch *Countdown* every afternoon |

# SURPRISE YOURSELF
# OCCASIONALLY

File Dizzee Rascal next to Dizzy Gillespie
in your record collection

Get in the car and see if you can do a
'shuffle' option on the satnav

Phone up Saga Holidays and ask for their
equivalent of an 18–30 holiday

# HOW TO MAINTAIN ENTHUSIASM

Find a bench by the ring road and sit
watching the commuters getting mad
with one another

Phone up your old boss at odd times of
the day to tell him you're having your tea
break now whether he likes it or not

Think of the happy smiling faces of your former colleagues still at work

Make yourself a 'to do' list each day but fill it with nice things like: '11.00 a.m. — coffee and a big slab of cake', '3.00 p.m. — stroll round the park and feed the ducks'

Go to the job centre and look at all the most horrible jobs you could be doing

# IMPORTANT THINGS TO REMEMBER

You don't have to undergo any high-powered job interviews again (unless you decide to apply for the post of collecting the trolleys at the local supermarket)

You're now free to do all the things you ever wanted to do — unfortunately you may now find yourself a bit too old to do them

The only excuse you now have for your house being untidy is that you are turning it into a piece of conceptual modern art

If you win the lottery now you won't have the satisfaction of telling your boss where to stuff his job

Retirement is a miracle cure — you will never again have a mystery 'illness' that requires you to have a day off work

# DO SOMETHING RETIRED PEOPLE AREN'T SUPPOSED TO DO

Don't shoot the breeze, shoot the rapids

Don't take up bridge; bungee jump
from one

Don't put a rug over your knees, cut a rug instead

Don't sit and vegetate, get up
and re-generate!

Don't put your feet up, have a knees-up!

# REASONS YOU SHOULDN'T VISIT YOUR OLD WORKPLACE

You'll be treated as an unpaid consultant ('Where did you put that important file just before you left?')

Half the people will say 'Who are you, then?'

You will be plunged into despair after seeing your incompetent assistant has been promoted to deputy director

# REMEMBER – THIS ISN'T A TRIAL RUN!

You're not going to get a call from the office asking why you've not come into work and realise that your retirement party was a hallucination

You've no longer got someone telling you what to do all day – unless you're married of course

You won't be sent back to work for another 40 years to build up your pension fund – or maybe that's not such a bad idea

It may be a bit late for a career change with a better pension at the end of it

Don't expect that round-the-world trip to book itself

Yes, it's finally here! This is it! Make the most of it!

# THINK POSITIVELY

It doesn't matter to you now if the
government decides to increase the
retirement age

You won't have to pay into your
pension any more!

Somebody else is now being driven mad trying to sort out your job (and/or the work you left behind when you retired)

www.summersdale.com